Index

I0475433

Overview

No matter what the year, no matter whether the world is having financial difficulties or untold wealth, everyone can always do more to better budget their money.

Some families have no clue about how to handle their money, some families have a lot of money and don't know what to do with and some families need to earn extra money and save at the same time.

The 50 different subjects in this book will aim to guide you on your way to creating additional funds, saving money and making the most of your income. I will even try to help you teach others, like your children how to manage their money giving them the best start in life and ensuring they are given the right information, learning the real worth of money.

I have put this book together in no particular order so it can be used as a reference whenever you want to pick it up. Each page can be read by itself and give a fully contained method which can be adopted by all ages.

Once you have read all the advice I give your eyes will be opened to a new way of thinking when it comes to money. My hope is that you will go on to find your own budgeting techniques more tailored to your own situation.

Thank you for purchasing this guide, may you learn to manage your money and most of all lead a more prosperous life.

John Stephen Geater.

Better Budgeting

A budget is basically a money plan, outlining your financial goals. Having a budget, you can well establish and regulate funds, set and achieve your financial objectives, and make advance decisions as to how you want your finances to function well for you.

The main idea in budgeting is for you to put aside a certain amount of money for expected as well as unexpected costs.

Simply put, budgeting means an estimation of monthly home expenses basing it on previous expenses and bills.

The initial step to take in budgeting is to find out how long will your compensation last. Define fixed expenses like car payments, home rental, insurance, etc. Likewise follow up your expenditures thoroughly for a month so you can discover and understand where your funds are going. Through proper determination of your "spending patterns", you can immediately identify solutions for effective budgeting.

For instance, when you have a steady monthly income of $4,000, you should subtract all your identified monthly bills from that income.

Other bills can be assessed and then subtracted from the amount of your income. The balance that remained after fixed costs can now be your budget in the household. Rather than allocating money for miscellaneous like gas, clothing, entertainment and groceries, financial planning will allow you instead to use proportions or percentages of it.

The strategic solution in order for budgeting to be successful is inflexibility as well as flexibility; there are fixed expenses so payment must be an inflexible factor.

Budgeting will best work when very scarce omissions are made to greater limits. The idea here is to formulate goals and plans, then abide by it as much as you possibly can.

Here are tips on how to budget:

1. Have good sense of money management. Your attitude is essential. Reach an agreement and compromise and know the significance of reducing expenditures; it all involves a lot of sacrifice.

2. Plan your situation. Make a listing with your earnings to one side and your overheads on the other side.

3. Know the difference between luxuries and necessities. List down what you believe as luxuries, with it, split the list in half, crossing out half the list.

4. Practice frugality but with dignity. You can have fun with little or without spending at all. Rather than going shopping, play with the kids at the beach or at the park.

Budgeting is an effective and fundamental tool that is readily available to everyone. Consider it, and benefit from it.

Budgeting Secrets

A Little Goes a Long Way: Smart Secrets to Budgeting

There's nothing more we want than to be able to efficiently manage our money. After all, the money that we want to manage is money that is oftentimes, hard earned. This is where a budget comes in. A budget executed properly, should help you see where your money is going, get more utility out of every buck, and help you save some extra for future use.

The first smart secret to a budget is to set a goal. What do you want to achieve? Do you want to correctly appropriate your income into bills payments? Do you want to put an amount aside for a big purchase or a huge investment? By having a goal, you will be able to shape your budget to best serve your interests.

Secondly, you would want to take note of where your money usually goes. This includes bills, major but regular purchases (like grocery costs, healthcare costs, and the like), and everyday miscellaneous purchases. Only when you list down where you know your money usually goes will you be able to identify which expenses you can do without. Once you've identified these regular expenditures, take into consideration what you can cut back on. How much do you spend on your daily caffeine fix in the morning? How much do you spend on newspaper deliveries to your front door? The measly $2 or $5 of these small purchases cumulatively translates to more than $3600 a year! Instead of buying your expensive latte or reading the newspaper on print, put aside the amount you would usually pay for these small routine purchases in a small container. You will be surprised at how much you're saving out of your older budget.

Being indebted is a vicious cycle on its own. You're talking about continuous payments, not to mention huge interest rates. The best way to deal with this is to pay the minimum on all of your debts in order to avoid paying extraneous late fees. Whatever cash excesses you may have, you can opt to add on to the payments you make in your biggest debt. This way, you are concentrated on getting the biggest debts first that cost you the greatest interest rates. Doing this progressively, you'll be amazed at how much you'll get off your huge debts.

The last and most important step is to jot down the amount you earn the sum you spend. You can make use of computer cash management programs, or make database sheets of your own. Make a system that works for you and will help you keep track of your monthly budgeting progress.

Budgeting Tools

Budgeting your monthly expenses in order to get the greatest return on your income (and perhaps, even put aside some for saving!) doesn't have to be extremely hard.

Various budgeting programs are available for use. Money management programs provide you with a usual package that allows you to enter your cash inflows and outflows, categorizes your expenditures, and at times, presents to you analysis of your spending behavior. Through these programs you can also input the various payments you have to make monthly, and subsequently track if you've paid your dues on time. Moreover, some programs also offer you a tax form draft that will help you make sure you're not missing out on any dues or any deductibles, for that matter.

Another budgeting tool that you can utilize are coupons. Various stores and magazines contain coupons that you can use to get discounts on various products. Should there be a need to purchase a particular product for which you have a coupon for, you will end up saving a fraction of what you might have had to spend on a regular purchase.

Lists—whether on a piece of paper, on your cellular phone, or on your personal digital assistant (PDA) will help you keep focused on what you have to buy, and in effect, keep track of the purchases you make. A classic example is your regular grocery trip. Prior to making the trip, plan out the week's entire menu and identify what food items and materials you need to purchase that are unavailable in your pantry. Then, make a list of other household items that you've run out of (or are eventually going to run out of before you can make the next trip to the grocery). Armed with these lists, you can go to the grocery and know exactly where to go and what you're going to buy. Without these lists, you will walk idly along aisles, and will likely pick up various food items that you won't likely need in the immediate future, or already have at home.

A filing system is perhaps one of the best budgeting tools you can have in your home. With simple, labeled file folders, you can put together your bills, your receipts, and whatever bank documents are issued to you when you save or pay. By putting together your bills, your credit card receipts, and the like, you are able to keep track of how much you owe and when your payments are due.

Effective budgeting tools are those that best address your needs as a consumer. Create your own budgeting tool or find a program to do it for you—just make sure it suits your lifestyle.

Choosing The Bank

When it comes to financial management, even business professionals reach a consensus as to what is the most effective, reliable, and secure means to manage your money, and that is through the bank. Your bank is an effective means to manage your bills payments, keep track of your transactions, receive your income and whatever extraneous cash inflow, and help you save effectively.

The last one is perhaps the most obvious feature of the bank that people do not take advantage of. A bank, being a financial intermediary, can actually help you save money efficiently. Here's how.

First, you are required to keep what is called a maintaining balance in your bank account. This means that even if you make deductions in your account, the bank requires you to save a bare minimum in order to continue enjoying their services. And yes, that translates to a forced saving on your part.

Another feature of bank saving is the fact that you are free to continuously add to your account whenever you can. Otherwise, your money will remain safe in your bank. Moreover, while it's staying in the bank, you are actually earning interest rates on your money.

What are savings interest rates? These are payments made by the bank to you for leaving your money in the bank. By depositing your money in the bank, your bank utilizes a portion of it in its loan operations where it subsequently earns through interest and loan charges. In effect, the income they receive trickles down to you, their source of money. This savings interest rate is actually an effective incentive system. Why so? If you save more money in your bank account through your deposits and savings, you end up receiving a higher return on the savings interest rate than other people would.

Banks have a threshold amount for you to be able to participate in the bank's long-term, higher yield savings schemes. Time-deposit accounts, mutual funds and the like require you to leave your money untouched for a longer period of time. In exchange for the bank's use of your money for a longer period of time, the percentages of interest return are double those that you would get in a regular savings account. You can add increments of a certain amount in order to increase the capital you invest in your time-deposit account or mutual fund. An increased account obviously translates to bigger interest gains.

Talk to your local bank about their savings schemes. They offer various mechanisms to encourage us consumers to entrust their money to them. In a bank, your money is in a safe place, and it is growing while it stays there.

Emergency Funds

Emergency funds are considered to be a necessity as far as financial security is concerned, since it can provide one with financial resources that one can resort to and depend on when an emergency arises such that when one is sick and have the burden of paying huge medical bills, or unexpected home or major car repair.

When one has no emergency fund, one can be obliged to acquire debt on your credit card that might take several years to repay with interest that would later cost so much more.

However by putting an extra thirty to fifty dollars every month in an individual "emergency savings account" one can be secured with what emergency the future may bring. In doing this, it is recommended that one regards the emergency fund as an additional bill, to be punctually paid each month.

Yes, one can and should budget and allocate the extra money for emergency fund, as this is very significant when one refers to his "financial future". Here, the goal is to create savings from budgeting your income; the emergency savings should ideally be equal to at least three months your living expenditures.

What's important is that you should steadily put a certain amount of money aside, and only use it for real emergencies.

Not like an investment, the success of one's long-term savings funds does not really count on the amount of return or interests but on placing a fixed amount of money away constantly and steadily so to have immediate access to it at all times.

In spite of one's financial status, the initial step in the process of constructing an emergency fund is by knowing where your money is presently being consumed or spent.

When one recognizes and determines where one's earnings are spent, then it will be easy for one to choose and make a decision where to trim down expenses. In other words, budget.

Budgeting is putting or setting aside money for anticipated and unanticipated future use. It is here that one sets up a goal so as to save. So set an emergency fund as your goal.

Checking, savings, money market accounts and "certificates of deposits", are great places to keep one's cash that might be needed on quick notice.

The amount saved from budgeting can either go to your savings goal, emergency fund or both. One could utilize the money saved from budgeting financial expenses by saving half of it to your savings account and half of it for emergencies. This way, you achieve your goals in savings and at the same time put in funds for emergency use. It's your choice.

Family Budget Saving

If you are in charge of creating the family budget, chances are, you've had the unfortunate experience of having a brilliant budget plan that isn't executed well. This happens to many families and couples, and with a little attitude tweaking, you can solicit the help of your family in making your budget work.

Create a family budget vision. Talk to your spouse and children about whatever budgetary constraints you are facing, or whatever financial goals you intend to set. By being completely honest about the bills and loans you have to pay, or your intention to save a certain amount of money for a family emergency fund (or a college fund, for that matter), you can help your family understand better your collective financial situation. This will allow them to change their perspective on purchases they make, and will help you make sure that whatever money crunching strategies you utilize won't be counteracted by a subsequent spree by your teen.

Another good technique is to create a list of usual expenditures per member of your family. Together, identify which items you can do away with in order to save up some extra money from your monthly income. By doing this altogether, you are making your family participate better and see the contributions they can make into making your family's finances better.

Should your child have the habit of continuously asking for money for minor and oftentimes unnecessary purchases, you can let your children learn to manage their own week's allowance. With their limited money to budget, they will realize the value of money.

Put a cap on the amount of expenditures you make in a week. The best way to do this is set aside a fixed amount of cash that you will spend for a week. By putting this limitation on your spending, you are forced to prioritize spending on the most essential over other things.

Make it easy for your family to save more. How often do you eat out? Most family budgets are blown over because of the frequency of dining out and the accompanying exorbitant expense of that activity. Eating at home will reduce your expenses, not to mention allow for your family to bond over cooking at home. Do you spend on routine purchases like coffee and newspapers? Cut back on the latte and the paper, and put aside the amount you would otherwise spend. Your family's collective saving will surprise you.

Lastly, don't be afraid to create a most efficient driving route, as well as grouping together activities into one car trip. This way, you can save a lot on time and even on gasoline and car expenses.

Flea Market Bargains

In the midst of all these skyrocketing prices, come the how's ways and means to save money and earn extra.

There are creative but practical ways you can engage in to help the family save and at the same time earn extra. The things that have been sitting in your attic for sometime and those that become all too familiar and useless might mean extra bucks. This way, it saves you space, cleaning materials and containers. This reduces maintenance expenses.

Garage sale at home is a save-and-earn endeavor for starters. Look at the success of flea markets where people can buy almost anything at a lower price but large amount of income for vendors.

How to maximize the potential of flea markets and bargain sales to help you save? Primarily, a flea market is a place where almost all who have something to sell can sell for tremendously lower costs but good quality items. If you have the right tools and enough preparation for a day's trip to a flea market, then you are ready to go with some handy tips:

1.　Ready your tools, maps, measurements and cash:
- easy-to-carry tool kit with screwdrivers, pliers, tape measure, pencil, ropes, set of swatches, paper and plastic bags and boxes;
- floor-plan measurements;
- maps, directions and phone numbers;
- bring enough cash and checks for high-priced items;
- dress yourself appropriately for bargain hunting.
2.　Early birds usually get the best selections.
3.　Keep a critical eye during shopping.
- Be ready to negotiate and haggle on the prices of items.
- Items sold here have greater possibilities, either you can redecorate or repaint them to make it look unique and attractive.

How to make this activity an earning endeavor? After your hands-on training in an established flea market, hope you took note of your observations and ideas; it is time to try out on your own.

Bear in mind five things crucial to garage sale success: location, date and time, variety of goods, organization/presentation, advertisements and prices.

- Spot a strategic location where people can access and drop by easily. Your house is the perfect venue for this. Weekends are the best to schedule your sale.
- During your cleaning session, take note of candidate items for the sale, label them (keep, for repair, must go) and give them a brand new look.
- Organize them well according to prices, use arrangement styles, decide on the tables, baskets and boxes for the items and decorate your venue with fabrics and other helpful materials.
- Lower your prices. The idea here is to dispose of the things but earn from them reasonably.

Frugality

The word "frugality" has left a more negative connotation for most people than simply being a saver, a cheapskate or tightwad. There is a thin line difference to saving and too much frugality to the point of being awkward and ridiculous. This is where the negative connotation comes from.

But if you are guided with the right principles and reasons in deciding to live a frugal life, you would never go wrong.

If you have decided to live frugally, no need to be worried of insults. Keep your head up high. And keep your focus through these tips.

1. Eating Out - Having gimmicks with friends on a Friday night is fine if you do it once in a while. But this can be expensive if you add them up at the end of the month.

2. Clothing - Naturally, if you are the kind of person who adores signature and designer clothes, do not expect that there will be something left of your take home pay. Instead of being trendy, wear clothes that can easily be matched with your other clothes.

3.   Own Home - If you are planning to move out and find a place to settle, do not be overwhelmed by the excitement, instead be practical. As a start, buy a smaller house or try other ways like rent-to-own, do-it-yourself arrangements, and owner financing.

4.   Buying Your Own Car - Shy away from sports cars or SUVs. Just stick to your purpose of buying a car which is to transport you anywhere you need to go. Check out also program cars like a new car warranty. Maybe this is not just the best time to replace your car with a new one.

5.   Shopping for Groceries - As much as possible do not go with items that are branded. Choose non-brands and try looking for items on the highest or lowest shelves for best prices. Grab the opportunity and shop during sales or use coupons.

6.   Family Out - There are inexpensive ways to bond with your family and be entertained like going to libraries, local parks, shopping, picnics, visit friends and local church.

7.   Buying School Supplies - Stock school supplies at home and do not buy anything fancy.

8.   Be contented with what you have and try to live within what you earn.

9.   Plan your Child's College Education - Teach them the ways to be independent and self-supporting by encouraging them to apply for scholarships and "on campus jobs".

10.   Be Aware of your Financial Limitations

11.   Anticipate your Failures by Planning - Have always a budget plan so you would avoid impulsive buying.

How Moms Save Money

Budgeting is truly the turf of most mothers. Aside from the traditional role imposed on mothers as the one who budgets the family finances, mothers have the instincts and foresights on what might happen in the future.

But how do moms really stretch the budget? She neither uses complicated formulas nor magic tricks but simple ingenuity and common sense. Peek in through moms' secrets in budgeting and learn. Role modeling is a good way to encourage attitude, especially towards money.

1. She clearly knows where all the money goes. Usually it goes to child care apart from the housing, health insurance, food and clothing. It is unlikely for her to cut cost on her children.

2. She studies all options given to her in terms of child care. Before she decides, she examines all aspects like safety, health and education.

3. To understand more, she talks to local child-care specialists and works out schedules with her employer for bonding time with kids.

4. For working moms, it is double the effort. They take care of the house and the children and at the same time work. She incorporates practical ways to accomplish both roles.

- Wearing professional clothes than trendy ones.
- Stays elegant but simple through a combination of basic colors.
- Dry cleaning costs a hefty amount, so, she dons on wash-and-wear clothes.
- Tone down on accessories.
- She engages in a lot of do-it-yourself habits like in cleaning spots and ironing wrinkles in her personal wardrobes.

5. Moms always shop with a list in her hand to keep track of her budget and expenses. She makes sure she does not

exceed. Also, she has no time for checking out tempting stuff at the shopping mall.

How To Budget Your Money

With prices of commodities increasing day by day it is proper to make your very own strategic plan on maximizing your financial resources and making sure that every penny earned is well spent.

Make your move on coordinating your finances and list of expenditures that may affect the way you use your income and empower you on your economic stability as a working individual.

Your source of income, lifestyle, spending habits, current job and house location, cost of living, payables and loans determines your level of budgeting needs. Starting to take charge of your finances is one sure way of becoming successful in a field of self-fulfillment and success.

The following tips and recommendations will provide you details on how you can help yourself manage your finances and assume a new outlook to become responsible in your spending.

- Treat Math As Your Lifetime Partner – Do the entire math in your purchasing needs. Try to compare prices across your current location for the price of a range of grocery and household items you need in a day-to-day basis.

- Save as much as you can in an item you are trying to buy. Chinese businessmen exercise effective buying techniques. They save as much as they can and usually purchase in bulk to increase their revenue index on the item they plan on selling as well.

- Gambling – Gambling tops the chart in making your life as chaotic as it could get. Gambling strips you off your finances and keeps you vulnerable from the threats of bankruptcy.

- Know Your Wants and Needs – Limit your spending on something which you are not in dire need of. According to a recent study, luxuries are second to gambling in terms of the degree of money-stripping capability.

- "Do Not Spend More Than you Earn" – Rags-To-Riches stories do not fail to mention this famous cliché. There is always truth to this phrase for you cannot live in a world where you consume more than what you can produce.

- Keeping A List – Making your own budget list is vital to your success to becoming prudent. A wise buyer needs to consider the amount of a certain commodity and how will it impact his life as an individual.

An un-conscientious consumer would not care about what is being purchased as long as he or she has money to buy for them. Unless you are someone who has a considerable amount of wealth and income resources, you can not afford to disregard this recommendation and go ahead with your practice.

How To Save Your Money

Saving is your best defense against bankruptcy. It insulates you from possible financial loss and gives you the ability to expand your finances and create a money-generating business machine that will help you earn extra.

Your potential to flexing your base income is augmented in ways that is not confined within the walls of basic employment. You can start up your own business, use it for loan purposes and earn interest on them while being used, among others.

But the basics of it all lies in saving – spending less than what you earn and keep something enough for future use and for unforeseen circumstances.

This article provides you with ways on how you can effectively maximize your financial resources and helps you manage your money by developing correct habits and outlook suitable for your goal.

- Wants and Needs – You buy items because you need them. A need is something you cannot take away from a person for these things are vital to his or her very existence and without them, they are categorically considered poor or deprived.

- Food, shelter, clothing and transportation are the primary examples. In a modern world, car and phone gadgets are a necessary part of a busy working individual. However, unless you are receiving more than $10,000 per month, you basically won't need to have a $40,000 to $50,000 luxury vehicle.

- The same is true for your telephone media. Having your own cellular phone is necessary but keeping up with the latest model or buying the all the latest releases are not practical and earns you more points on plunging into a staggering financial downfall.

- Less Is best – Extravagance is the rule of the kings. While we sometimes need to afford a little affluence in terms of the food we eat, the body pampering devices and accessories, such as clothes and body-relaxing services, we also need to consider that these types of activities should only be reserved for special occasions and for cases when you have some excess left in your household budget.

- Spend Less; Save More – Spending more than what you earn or produce is a bad habit that most people get used to doing everyday.

Allocate a special percentage of your earnings to go into your savings accounts while spending the rest for your day-to-day expenses.
Unexpected charges, such as the visitation of your relatives or a house party due to a certain celebration will be there to stay so you need not make some leeway budget on them and save them should situation not arise.

Importance Of Saving Money

The value of money cannot be underestimated. In a recent national survey, more than 96% Americans agreed that early monetary savings would help one achieve a fruitful and stable life.

Saving is a way of insulating oneself from the many symptoms of health and natural adversity. While an average youth of yesteryears thinks more about short-term financial goals such as purchasing a new pair of signature shoes, owning a new jet ski or a brand new car, statistics show that more and more are starting to realize the importance of keeping a personal savings.

Long terms goals are described as goals that have a lasting effect should a person's present actions be religiously maintained.

The following statements are outlined to provide information and tips on how you can start up your money-saving gimmicks and ensure a happy and financially stable future and list the reasons as to why saving money should occupy a greater place in our list of priorities in life.

Reasons for Saving:

- Saving for your Future and Present Needs – Saving today will provide you with flexible financial resources in the future.

- Keeping at least 20% of your monthly earnings while using the other for your household, personal and unexpected expenses will surely play a big part in your pursuit for a stable future.

- Saving for an Investment Need – Savings can also be a source of your future capital for engaging in business enterprises.

- It will provide you more opportunity for venturing on your unexplored talents and earn you a huge potential in increasing your money exponentially.

- Saving for your Retirement – More than 23% of today's elderly were shown to have failed in one instance in their lives, to save and strategically used their money for preparing their way to retirement. As a result, these folks extend their entire retirement career working on an equally satisfying job that pays them enough to cover their basic expenses.

Keys to Fulfilling your Saving Goals:

No matter how good our intentions and objectives for saving are, we should also take note that goals can fall and touched the following baselines or characteristics.

- Attainability – Goals should be something attainable and one which can be achieved without you doing something extraordinary or illegal. A little amount of patience and hard work are key.

- Consistency – Changing your goals from time to time due to incidents that may arise in the near future are sure ways to deterring your intention to save.

While we need to focus on the present incidents, we also need to take hold of our original intention and continue until you have gained enough leads to get it.

Listing All Your Expenses

With the institution of malls, affordability of technology, and rising cost of health care, loans, and rising inflation, it has become very difficult for one to spend less and save money for future use.

Current statistics show that banks are showing a considerable decline on each bank account holder's savings and have shown an increased in the number of withdrawals per month leaving people little money to spend before the next salary strikes their account.

Along this fact shows a relative increase in the amount of spending made in private institutions marketing different products.

While these facts and a host of temptations are a commonplace scenario in the real world, there are many ways by which you can keep yourself from getting into the hype and aid you in creating and developing your personal and unique habit of saving a few dollars from your basic salary.

- Compulsive Buying – Given enough money, 7 out of 10 people lure into the idea of buying a personal item they like in a store at a first glance.

- In a simulated sociological study, people who originally planned on window-shopping ended up buying personal stuff if they are taking their personal bankcards with them.

  If you are doing window-shopping, limit your spending to a few bucks and try making your list the next time you plan on buying such items. Buy only the store items you need and abandon those that do not satisfy an immediate need.

- Budgeting – Along with your pursuit to saving money, it is also important to keep an organized and effective, yet reasonable budgeting technique. Budgeting eliminates buying temptations that would tend to build up during malling and help you save money along the process due to preformed lists of items you need to buy.

- Performing Price Comparison – The World Wide Web provides a great avenue on providing a checklist of prices on specific items that you plan on buying.

  This is great for you if you are into bulk buying and plan on conducting your shopping activity in one place. This will give you a good idea if the usual store from where you usually get all your everyday household needs provides you a reasonable price for specific products.

- Take All the Convenience At Home – Lunch, snacks, and major meals are something which you can. prepare at home. If you are serious on saving money, you can prepare all this from home and get away with some amenities of the gut by replacing soda with water. This is not only beneficial to your pocket but does a great deal for your health as well.

Method Of Saving Money

Saving is basically putting aside money or a way to utilize your present income for future use.

One saves for several reasons such as for a college education, buying a new car, for a new TV set you wish to acquire in three to four months time, for down payment on a home, or to provide for yourself when retirement comes.

As much as there are several reasons for saving, there are likewise many methods in which one can save. In most instances, the best method can be determined by whatever plans you have for the future.

1. Savings accounts. When saving for just a short period or for emergency purposes, consider opening a savings account passbook, as it is in this method that you can easily gain access to your funds.

   Great for both long and short term savings, you can deposit and withdraw money to your account and earn interest, based on your average daily balance. A minimum balance is required to be maintained though, and you are charged with a penalty should you fail to maintain it.

2. Checking account with interest. Here one can benefit from checking account conveniences, while your deposits gain interests. Generally these types of accounts grants privileges such as limitless withdrawal and check writing, access to ATM and bill payments that can be done online.

This method typically requires a daily maintaining balance of at least $2,000.

3. Money market insured accounts. For long-termed goals, this method is ideal, as it generally offers a much higher rate of interest compared to a regular or standard savings account.

    The interest rate usually is dependent on the amount of money in your bank account; larger balance means higher interest.

4. "CD" or Certificates of Deposit. This is a savings method requiring you to "loan" your money to your financial agency for a certain time frame, usually ranging from thirty days up to five years. Here, the longer the time span again, means higher interest.

    Keep in mind that usually insurance companies offer better deals on interests compared to banks, so before you invest, compare rates first!

At certain times, when your goal is many years away, it can be a wiser decision to save money in a certain way that you are not drawn on using it other than the main reason for saving it. Deciding on the right financial agency such as a bank, credit union or insurance firm can bring about a lot of benefit in your finances.

Modern Ways To Save

Saving has always been a way of life for people who believed on its power. These people know that they have to save more money in order to create a more established future.

However, as time goes by, more and more people find it hard to save money. They contend that saving is no longer a way of life but a resolution that they have to strictly adhere to just to salt away some amount of money.

Some people even insist that it is no longer possible for a person to save more money because most of them are already living paycheck to paycheck. With all the high-prices of commodities these days, saving more money is no longer workable.

But the point is that people can indeed save more.

How? Here is a list of some modern ways that will let you save more money:

1. Save some percentage from your salary

Most money-savers automatically take at least 30% from their salary and save them into their savings account. The basic concept here is that most of us spend whatever amount we have on our paycheck, and maybe even more. If you are able to limit that amount, your expenses will unexplainably get smaller.

2. Pay everything in cash

Credit cards had always been a way of life for most consumers. The problem is that they become so comfortable with it that they tend to spend everything on credit. In fact, statistics show that the average family has an average outstanding balance on their credit cards amounting to $7,000. And they even pay almost $1,000 in each year just on the interest charges alone.

Hence, because of this comfortable shopping, they forget to keep track of their expenses and accumulate more payables than what they can afford to pay.

3. Set goals

Create goals that you really want and not be fickle-minded about it. If there's a certain amount involved, be specific with the amount, like saying "I will save $5,000 in a year and not around $5,000."

Try to set your goals based on your priorities. Have a period for every goal.

4. Check your company's retirement plan

With your employer plan such as the 401(k) or the 403(b), you can definitely save more money for the future. Here, your company will deduct a percentage of your salary from each paycheck and invest the amount in your choice of instruments—mainly mutual funds.

The bottom line is that saving is not just a way of life or a resolution. It's the ultimate gratification that you get as a fruit of your labor.

Money Budgeting Software

The problem with most people these days is that they get so comfortable with their expenses through the aid of credit cards. They become so indulged with cashless shopping that more and more people are spending more than what they can afford.

For this reason, experts contend that budgeting can definitely alleviate the consumers from "financial strain" by managing their expenses and income instead of falling into the pit of liabilities.

However, some people just contend that they cannot simply do budgeting alone. They insist that they need some help in order to come up with a reliable and workable budget.

That's why some financial experts have created some money budgeting software that will facilitate the creation of a good budget in order to promote wise money-saving strategies.

Basically, money budgeting software assists an individual in his or her expenditures and uses the money sensibly. These new technologies will help distribute the money into various aspects and areas and will also help add to savings.

So, if you still don't know what the money budgeting software can do for you, here is a list of its advantages:

1. It helps you keep track of your expenses

Money budgeting software can definitely allow you to keep track of your expenses. With this kind of technology, you get to understand your cash flow and allow you to be aware of how much money you spend and earn.

2. It helps you to create some probable projections of the future

While some people are comfortable with the usual type of budgeting on paper, utilizing a money budgeting software can give you more than what you expect. You can even make some possible projections using your integrated money budgeting software. And if you are really into hard copies, you can even print them out for record keeping.

3. It gives you control

The problem with most people who do not have a budget to guide them is that they tend to overspend with what they have.

With this kind of help, you can gain control of your expenditures. You will be able to know when you are already overspending or not. Plus, you become attentive of the blow of every money decision that you make.

The bottom line is that money budgeting software can definitely give you the kind of assurance and control that you need to keep track of your expenses. In this way, you can be surer that all of your spending activities are based on reason and plan and not just sheer indulgences.

Money Saving Coupons

One great irony of life is that people find it so easy to spend money and yet, they find it doubly hard to save money.

Almost 80% of the consumers, according to some surveys, tend to spend their money easily and find it hard to save even just 10% of their income or any amount of their earnings. They always insist that they have more expenses than they can handle; that is why it is so hard for them to really create a hefty amount for savings.

What people do not know is that they can easily save more money even on their daily expenses if they just know how to do it.

The point is that if they were really wise consumers, they would definitely take advantage of freebies and discount items that can absolutely cut their expenses almost in half.

One of the best examples is the utilization of money saving coupons.

The problem is that many people are still not aware of the benefits that money saving coupons can give. They contend that these freebies just offer such a little amount of money and that they can be better off without it.

Therefore, for those who are not yet fully aware of the benefits they can derive from these money saving coupons and what they can do in order to save more money, here is a list of some of tips on how to use these coupons for a cause:

1. Look for the right places

If you are not yet aware of the right places where you can get excellent money saving coupons, try to look in your local newspaper, especially the Sunday editions. It's one of the best places where you can get discount coupons.

Usually, different establishments provide discount coupons to entice consumers to buy their products. That's why they use the paper to distribute their freebies.

2. Shop online

Online businesses also provide money saving coupons. What people do not know is that online discount coupons provide more money saving percentage than what the newspapers can give.

Best of all, it is so easy to accumulate discount coupons. All you have to do is to sign up for the online business and you can easily get some of their freebies.

3. Coupons are great money savers

The very advantage of money saving coupons is that they can cut your bill to almost 50%.

Indeed, using money saving coupons can definitely save you more money than what you have expected. So, for those who do not know this yet, try to cut more coupons and start saving.

Money Saving Ideas

Want to save money but don't know how? Feel like depriving yourself when it comes to saving money? Don't be disheartened. Try these five money saving ideas, without breaking up a sweat!

Reduce or eliminate magazines. If you are a typical American family, your mailbox gets its regular fill of magazines: business, sports, home and garden magazines. Can you imagine how much each of these subscriptions cost? Annually, it is an average of about $20 per magazine. If your family is subscribed to 5 different magazines, that's already $100 savings per year! If you still need the information from such mags, try to check out their websites and you'll be surprised at how much free information is available!

Buy in bulk. How can warehouse and discount clubs drastically lower their prices? Because they buy and sell in bulk. And so should you! Consumables that are non-perishable can be purchased 10-15% cheaper when bought in bulk. Be sure to stock up only on fast-moving items such as kitchen towels, cleaners, canned goods, etc., to avoid wasting money on rancid food.

Eat at home. Eating out has become an American lifestyle. What used to be an activity to celebrate special occasions has become part of the daily, fast-paced life. But did you know that eating out could chomp as much as 40% of your budget for food? That's as much as $40 weekly, saved just by eating in!

Plan your meals. Eating out 4X a week need not be your solution to a dynamic lifestyle. Menu planning is! Take time on weekends to plan for the following week's meals. Every night, before you hit the sack, take out the ingredients for the meals of the next day from the freezer, and store them in the refrigerator. By the time you get home from work, everything is thawed and ready to be cooked. And because eating out is part of the American way of life, you would have saved enough money to spend for dining out on special occasions!

Homemade skin care. Is your dermatologist eating up your budget? Don't you wish you can be beautiful and save money at the same time? The answer is yes, you can! By using ingredients from your pantry, you can take care of your skin and still save a fortune. Try the following:

- Honey and oatmeal can exfoliate dry skin.

- Ginger seeped in a bath softens your skin.

- Cucumber and milk softens tired skin.

Without drastically changing your lifestyle, you have started your path on saving money. Secure your future by using these money saving ideas, today!

Money Saving On Food

Thinking of cutting down your expenses on food? Then you should read the following tips. They will surely help you on reducing your food expenses. They are by no means comprehensive but they will be very useful.

For coffee drinkers

It is a good idea to re-use the grounded coffee once. Using coffee grounds two times or more will not greatly affect the taste of the coffee. It is highly encouraged to do this using a filter that is permanent and avoid the paper variety. Keep the grounds refrigerated until using it the following day.

For bread lovers

Grocery stores sell bread that was made the day before at a much lower price. There is nothing wrong with eating bread that was made the day before since it still is good to eat. If you have a lot of space in your refrigerator, store a lot for bigger savings. If you will eat the bread, you can defrost it using your microwave oven. Re-heat it every 30 seconds to prevent the edges of the bread from getting too hard.

When buying from the grocery

Before going to the grocery, you should have already made a list of all the things that you really need. Prioritize basic goods and avoid buying things that you do not really need. Observe the prices indicated on the displays. Remember, branded products cost considerably more than store brands. It is also a good idea to keep the receipt of your previous trip to the grocery and make it as a basis for your purchases on your next trip. To have higher savings, buy more of the product. You can always store it in your refrigerator or in the house to minimize your trips to the grocery store.

When eating outside

If you are going to eat in a pricey restaurant, the best time for you to go there would be during lunch. Food during lunch usually costs less and this will be to your advantage. When staying at the hotel on your trips, it is a good idea to check if they also include breakfast in your total room charge. You should also find out where the locals eat. Chances are, they will eat where the food is great and the price is even better. When going around, carry with you some snacks. A chocolate bar, chips, and cookies will go a long way while strolling around.

Eating cheaply does not necessarily mean eating bad food. Look around and you will be suprised at the options you can choose from. Take time and consider your choices so that you will not only eat a lot but save some money also.

Patience And Saving Money

Patience is a virtue. It takes some character to exhibit such levels of moral excellence, but did you know that by doing so, you could save money at the same time? Read on to find out how you can economize by emanating the virtue of patience.

Have the patience to walk instead of drive. It saves you gas, parking and the stresses of driving. Walking improves your health and well being while saving gas money.

Be patient: compare before you buy. From personal clothing to health club memberships, from plumbing services to insurance plans, from car accessories to a new home; compare the offers of 3 to 5 suppliers or service providers before finally settling with one. Let them know that you are taking the time to search the market and they may just be able to offer you the best savings. Truly, the patient consumer is a winner!

Use coupons as much as possible. Be patient in cutting them out and going through them before making any purchase. Pack them together with your grocery bag or in the car so you can use the discount voucher at every opportunity. One can save $20 - $50, just by using the coupons.

Track your expenses. Have the patience to keep your receipts and record all your expenses, no matter how small or frequently they occur. By doing so, you are made aware of where every single penny goes. Furthermore, you will know when you have spent too much on clothing, when in fact you still need to settle your credit card balance, or pay the mortgage. You will have a better hold of your financial health, by patiently tracking your finances.

Hold-off and sleep on it! If you are about to purchase a $100 item, hold off the purchase until you've given it much thought, say sleeping on it for 1-2 nights. If after such time, you decide that you absolutely need and can afford the purchase, then go ahead. Nevertheless, you'll be surprised at how much you can save by just sleeping and thinking things over.

Devote money in long-term investment. Understand that when you take up long-term investment, you do not need the money for now, and it is not considered as part of your daily finances. However, such money when set-aside will reap great rewards in the future.

Exude moral excellence by patiently saving for years to come, starting today!

Practicalities Of Saving Money

Saving money is not as hard as it seems. Here are ten practical tips that you can do to begin saving money, without changing your lifestyle.

1. Replace incandescent bulbs with compact fluorescent (CFL) bulbs. CFL bulbs consume 80% less energy than incandescent bulbs, but give the same illumination. Make sure to buy only lamps and bulbs that have the Energy Star rating to ensure quality compliance.

2. Make a list when going to the grocery and stick to it! Anything that is not on the list is not a "need", but merely a "want" so avoid busting your pockets for unnecessary items. Buy non-perishable consumables in bulk to benefit from bulk discounts.

3. Use coupons when available. Take the time and have the patience to clip and organize grocery coupons. When added together, savings from using all coupons in one grocery trip can be as much as $20-$30. Purchase dining and shopping coupons online and print them at home. Doing so can save you at least 50% on the face value of the coupons.

4. Buy online, whenever possible. Online stores pass their savings from rental costs and warehousing to the online consumer, thus they can afford as much as 70% off their rack price. When buying items online, Google it first together with the word, "discount code". This can give you further reductions on the item you want to purchase. Try also online bidding: they offer at least 75% off the original purchase price, for practically new (slightly used!) items.

5. Take lunch to work. Buy potato chips and soda from the grocery and make a homemade sandwich and pack them in a brown bag.

6. Eat homemade dinners as often as possible. Plan menus that are practical and easy-to-cook to encourage eating at home. Save money by dining out only on special occasions.

7. Use everyday pantry items for skin and body care. Cucumbers, honey, milk, lemon, salt and baking soda are some items in your home that can also be used to take care of your skin.

8. Avoid shopping to de-stress. Try walking around the park or watching a movie instead.

9. Bring your own sodas and snacks when watching a movie. The cost of sodas and snacks are at least 25% higher in movie houses. Plus, homemade popcorn tastes much better: you can put on all the salt and butter you want!

10. Pay off your credit card balances each month and avoid finance charges. Better yet, use cash as much as possible, unless using plastic will give you a better deal (0% interest on appliance purchases, or cash rebates).

Priorities Of Budgeting Money

Often times, the family budget is a source of conflict. Most of the time, the major earner makes the final financial decision, which isn't always a welcome deal for the rest. Since money is such an intrinsic part of family life, families need to achieve accord in this aspect. There is a four-step cycle in budgeting the family money to maintain peace and harmony.

1. Set your priorities.

Priorities are different from goals. They are aspects in your family's life that you, as a family, want to set focus on, say health or children's future. While goals are specific targets that support priorities.

In setting priorities, do not set too many as it defeats the purpose. Ideally, there should only be one, but because life is not ideal, 2 to 3 are reasonable.

As the priorities are set and agreed upon, write them down. Post the paper where everybody can see them to remind them of what your family is focused on for the next few years.

2. List down your goals.

Once the family has set and agreed on priorities, the next step is to set the goals. Goals are specific and measurable conditions that, when achieved, will support the priorities.

In setting goals, establish a target that is both challenging yet achievable. A 10-15% of the family's income is a good savings target for a child's future education: stretching yet reachable.

Try to limit your family into setting 1-2 goals per priority, to maintain focus.

3. Work towards your goals.

After setting your priorities and goals, start living by them. All of the family's activities will be geared towards working at your goals. Track progress, particularly on financial goals, by using an income and expense-tracking tool. The simplest way is to get a notebook and list down all expenses and incomes and set a budget for future spending. There are those that invest in computer software or a family accountant. Whatever it is, the important thing is to have a system of monitoring the family's performance towards achieving their goals.

4. Evaluate your family life.

At a certain point in time, when you feel like it's time to evaluate your life, check how your family is doing against the goals. Goals that have been achieved can be checked off the list, and new ones can be formulated.

At times, in major changes, say a career move, or when a family member goes away, it may be time to re-evaluate priorities. When such a time comes, then the cycle begins, just like what it's for: life!

Save Money On Credit Cards

Having a credit card is very convenient since carrying a lot of cash becomes unneccesary and you might even have a hard time leaving your credit card at home. But with its advantages comes also its disadvantages. Since you can always buy things without carrying cash around, you are always tempted to buy something that you come across. If you have excellent control on your finances then good for you. If you have a hard time managing your credit card, then these pointers can help you.

Get organized

First thing's first, obtain your credit card records to have a better idea of your spendings. Be sure to double check the records for errors and ensure its accuracy. A good example would be to find out if you have outstanding debts that should not be there as well as the accuracy of the listing of your former and present address.

Evaluate your credit card

Go over your recent credit card records and look at the interest rates. Some credit card companies have promos wherein they offer lower interest rates for a period of time and this promo may already be over yet you have no idea and are already paying at a higher interest rate. Also take note of the membership fee which they charge annually since some have very high membership fees. Consider cancelling this if you are not using it frequently.

Pay on time

It is important to pay your bills on time since it can have a negative effect on your credit record or rating. You will also be able to avoid getting charged because of not paying on time. Try asking the credit card company to remove the overdue charge if you have forgotten to pay it on time for the first time.

Manage your debts

If you see that you have more debt than what is comfortable, think ahead and plan out how you will repay it or at least reduce your debt. Devise a way to pay more than what is required of you so that you will have a reduced payment schedule. Prioritize the card that has the highest interest rate. Do not bring your credit card always when you go around since temptations abound.

Don't bite more than you can chew

As the saying "don't bite more than you can chew" goes, do not spend more than you can afford. True, a beautiful gold bracelet may be enjoyable to wear but its price tag may mean paying a lot for the next months. If you are bent to save money when using your credit card, unnecessary items like jewelry and the like should be at the bottom of your considerations.

Save Money On Gas

The price of gasoline is on the rise. This is truly a great concern if you are following a tight budget. So how can you save some money on gas? Read these tips.

The carpool system

This is a great idea for employees and students alike. Since all of you will have the same destination, there is no need to bring extra vehicles if you can all fit in one car or van. If you are with your co-workers, it is a good idea to bring your cars alternately or on rotation. If you have children that you bring to school or social events, exchange driving responsibilities with your friends.

Commute to work

You can always take the public transportation system when going to the office. This is also a good way to relax since you are not driving. You can even take a short nap while on your way.

Look at the prices of different gas stations

Take time to drive around and check the pump prices of the gas stations near your neighborhood. Keep in mind that a few cents difference can add up to a lot if you continually have your car re-filled in the same gas station all the time.

Shed some sweat

A good way to save money on gas and keep yourself healthy at the same time is by walking or riding a bike to your destination. It saves time since you do not have to look for parking and also makes you healthier from the exercise. Utilizing these alternatives will also keep you from getting stuck in traffic which will surely waste a lot of your time and gas.

Keep your car in very good condition

It is necessary to keep your car's engine in good running condition so that it will not consume a lot of fuel. When driving around on errands, plan out your route before you even get out of the house. This will minimize your trips going back and forth. If is also ideal to use the aircon as minimal as possible since it drastically increases the car's fuel consumption.

Check your car's tire pressure

Keep it a habit to check your car's tires so each one has the right amount of pressure. Having unequal pressure can greatly affect the car's fuel economy. It is also advised for you to refrain from accelerating too fast since this means burning a lot more fuel.

These are some of the things that you can do to save on gas. Gasoline is not a renewable resource, therefore using it wisely is very important to conserve this valuable commodity.

Save Money On Groceries

 Saving Money is one hard task. There are lots of things to be considered, primarily on how to budget your cash on hand that would somehow, if not manage to have excess left money, be exact of what it should be used for. Budgeting is really a pain in the neck. Allocation of electric bills, water bills, phone bills, etc. is just few of the many things being considered on how to utilize your cash wisely. Food is no exception. Being the most important of all house responsibility, we prioritize on how to budget our money, reducing the money spent without sacrificing the food allocation. We mainly buy necessities in groceries. It would be of help if you list down goods you have to buy together with their prices (if possible) so as to ensure yourself that the budget allotted for food is exact or there is a shortage. If so, you could trim down your list or think of a better replacement. To furthermore avoid shopping shortages, here are some tips.

- List goods that should always be found in the. kitchen. Examples of which are coffee, milk, sugar, soy sauce, vinegar, salt, onion, garlic. These goods are necessary, so they are always being bought.

- Plan your weekly meals ahead of time. This would avoid you overspending on goods invaluable or missing some ingredients that are needed. This would not just clear your worries but it would also save your time.

- Don't buy branded goods; instead choose a product that has the same quality of those expensive goods. You'll get the same benefit without spending more.

- Buy goods that have dual purpose. A good example of which is mayonnaise. You can use it as a sandwich spread or make macaroni salad instead. In a way, you could enjoy eating both without spending too much.

- Buy less expensive cuts of meat. List recipes that the cuts won't matter. At least, you won't be sacrificing the taste of the food and at the same time you'll have the chance to buy a larger quantity.

- Pay in cash. You might be tempted to buy unnecessary goods. This would avoid you from going over your card limit.

- Try to be inventive and creative at the same time. Leftovers could be precooked in a way that it would look appealing again to your appetite.

- Bring some snacks whenever you travel. This could be a good reliever for your hunger along the way and chances of being tempted to stop in a mini store; if not be impossible, at least be lessen.

- Keep a list of prices of goods you always buy. At least, with those products you're sure of how much you'll be spending and you could do just a small amount on goods you wish to buy.

- Shop only once or twice a month. In that way, less time will be spent on going to a grocery store and at the same time, chances of overspending will be minimized.

Save Money On Utilities

Expenses on utilities contribute to most of your household bills. Did you know that you could save a lot of money through your utilities? Here are some pointers to help you do this:

1. Identify which appliances consume much electricity and contribute the most in making the electric bill cost that much. You can save hundreds of dollars annually by enrolling in a home management load program that offer a 100-dollar savings in a year on electric utility hour rate programs. This will help you lower your electric payments and will teach you on home energy conservation.

2. It is recommended that you have improved appliance efficiency. The heating system appliances are the ones that consume too much electricity. The refrigerator and the water heater consume that much energy as well. Make sure to check these items regularly to ensure their efficiency. A well-maintained appliance will sustain its performance and will give you it's accurate use of electricity.

3.   Always remember to give your furnace a tune up at least twice a year. You have to cover the water heater to insulate it and give your refrigerator coils a cleaning at least twice a year as well. You may also set a timer for the heater to have regular flow of electricity whenever it is in use. You may call your utility service to check if there is a low rate offered during any specific time of the day.

4.   You may also save money by lowering your heating bills. You may set your thermostat down three degrees to make you save 3 percent on your bills. You may even save more by not using it while you are at work or you can even turn it lower during night time when you are asleep. This can help you conserve electricity and save more money.

5.   You may want to lessen your long distance telephone calls to lower your telephone bills. If it is a need to call a very important person, you may call during weekends and night hours. Telephone companies offer a lower rate for long distance calls during those times of the day. The best alternative to save money is by using the Internet to communicate with your friends and relatives instead of the telephone.

6.   You may want to consider lowering your water bills in order to save money. Check if there are leaks so that you may fix them immediately. You may put a water saving showerhead to lessen the use of water when taking a shower. You can use a big container to stock water in the bathroom as an alternative rather than using the shower in the bathroom.

Saving Money Tips

In this world today, prices seem to go higher every year. Saving money can sometimes be a hard job for many people. To help you save money, here are some pointers for you:

1. Determine the things that are important to you. Identify the items that you need and the items that you want to have. Always remember that you should only buy things that are important and needed in your lifestyle.

2. Make sure that you spend your money only on basic needs like food, transportation, shelter, and clothing. These basic needs are worth spending for because these are important for your health and security. They are the things that you cannot live without and should be allotted in your budget.

3. Make a list of the things that you want to buy and be sure that the items that you are buying are good enough to sustain your basic needs. You have to be satisfied with the things that you have now, as long as it is still useful and can accommodate your needs.

4. You may avoid unwanted purchases by trying the item first before buying it. This is to make sure that the item is worthy enough to acquire. There are instances that you tend to buy things without even knowing its effectiveness and quality. You have to keep in mind that you always need to spend your money wisely on items that have quality and are according to your budget.

5. You may try to budget your money in advance. You can make a plan first before spending your money. There are instances that you spend your money without even thinking that it is not the right time to have it. It also advisable to buy items at the end of the season, prices at this time of the year are low and cheap.

6. You may compare items on their prices. Do not limit your options to just one store only. You may find the best item that can be useful and affordable to you by window-

shopping first rather than buying by impulse. Many stores out there carry the same items and can offer lower prices.

7.   You can save more money in your household by conserving electricity. Be sure to turn off appliances that are not in use. You may compare your monthly electric bills regularly to check if you are maintaining your desired bill.

8.   You can save on your transportation by traveling wisely. It is recommended that you make your itinerary to help you to not forget your destinations. Being organized will help you save money and time

Save Money While Shopping

Shopping is very addictive. Most of the time, the household budget is sacrificed once you go shopping. Shopping should not give you headaches as long as you know how to budget. Here are the things that you need to remember:

1.   Always remember to spend your money wisely whenever you go shopping. Bring only the exact amount of money you need in buying your items. To ensure that you only buy the important things, you have to make a list of the items that you need to buy. You may then budget your money wisely and will prevent you from buying things that are not that important.

2.   It is advisable that you compare prices from different stores before buying an item. Do not limit yourself to just one store. There are stores that offer the same quality but can have a lower price. A smart thing you may do is to be attentive to the prices of the items that you buy regularly when shopping. There are instances that a store has an untimely changing of prices on different items.

3.   It is recommended that you do your shopping during the end of the season. Prices of many items, especially clothes, are very low and affordable during this time of the year. You may buy clothes in the months of August and

September if you are looking for bargain clothes for your summer wear.

4.   You may shop in dollar stores where you can find items that are on sale and where prices are low. Although the quality of some items is not the same when you buy in malls and shopping galleries but the merchandises are still new and not yet used. These stores can provide you the best prices that can cope with on your budget.

5.   Another way to save money while shopping is to economize the travel you make in finding the stores you want to buy an item. You may take a stop on your daily route to check if the items you buy regularly have not changed their prices or are still in the price of your budget. You may purchase the item even before you do your shopping schedule. This can save you fuel and time.

6.   Try to find discount stores that offer quality items that have discounts and can offer a very affordable price on your desired item. The prices on discount stores may vary depending on the season of the year. These stores can be located in large shopping areas like in malls and shopping galleries.

Save Money With Transportation

Prices go higher every year, especially the cost of gas. Transportation is one big factor that makes the household budget difficult to cover all your expenses. Here are some guidelines to help you save money from transportation:

1.   To save money, you must always check on your vehicle regularly. A well-maintained vehicle can get you out of trouble on repair expenses. You can actually spend only $50 on maintaining your vehicle and save up to $800 on repair costs in a year. You can even save more if you do the maintenance yourself and not bring your car into an auto shop.

2.   If you want to save more money, it is recommended not to buy a new car. The value of a car depreciates automatically when you drive it out off the showroom of the car dealer shop. You may buy a car that is used at least one year. It will save you thousands of dollars to the actual worth of the car when it was new. The owner will then pay all the depreciated value of the car.

3.   Save money on buying used cars by comparing the prices of the car dealer and the actual price on the list of the used car dealer ads. To ensure the car that you buy is well conditioned, you may ask for the help of a mechanic to check if the car is good enough for its price. It is better to buy a used car from a person you know and trust. This will help you make sure that you have a good deal in acquiring a car.

4.   Try to compare gasoline rates. You may refuel your car with the gasoline station that offers the lowest price on gasoline. You can even save more by pumping gas yourself and use the lowest octane in your car's manual. It is also recommended that you pay cash than credit cards that charge extra rates. Do not forget to check the gas cap if it is tightened to ensure no gas is spilled out.

5.   Always keep your engine tuned-up and have your tires inflated to their desired pressure to save you more money. A well-maintained engine consumes less gas. Keep your car's trunk clean to save more fuel. Heavy loads in your vehicle can consume more fuel because of the excess weight it carries.

6.   Try to limit the use of your car on your daily route. You may take the bus or the subway to save gasoline. You can also save time by ignoring the traffic that you encounter everyday on the streets.

Saving Money And Banking

Have you reached the point when merely looking at your bank statements you get a headache already? You might find your records out of place. You might even find yourself lost as to your current status and accounts. However, this is not a point for you to simply fret.

Now, you have to take the matters to your own hand.

Saving Money

Saving money is an important matter. It is something that you have to do regularly to come up with a considerable amount. With the current trends of the economy and the widespread consumerism, it has to be part of your lifestyle as it is your way to ensure a brighter future.

Banking

Most people who really want to save would maintain a savings account in a bank rather than put it in a money box or under a pillow at home. Putting the money in the bank is really a prudent move. The money is in safekeeping. It is not within your immediate reach, thus it is not within your immediate disposal. It can even earn interest.

Banking Strategy for More Savings

This means organizing your finances. This is where you look at your status, plan ways to improve your standing and make terms work for your benefit.

Savings Account

Having a savings account is definitely a sure way of getting assistance in your pursuit to save. However, you must be doing the right thing. Your money must really stay there. You actually have to maintain a certain amount to earn interest with your account.

If you cannot keep yourself from withdrawing, hide your ATM card. This defeats your goal to save and too many withdrawals will incur you fees.

Long-Term Deposits

Should it prove difficult to keep your savings account balance intact, you can opt to long-term deposits. This is where a certificate of deposit is given to you in exchange of a certain amount of your money. You can get higher interest rate here, so your money can earn more. You are also not allowed to get back the money within a certain period or else you have to pay a fine. The fine should be deterrent enough to keep from spending.

Features and Offers

Identify among the various banks out there. Consider the features they provide to clients. One bank will offer higher interest rates although you may feel more secure with another bank. Some also give special offers for a certain period. Simply know your options and study the information carefully before making a decision.

Saving Money And Credit

You have long known the credit card. It is said to be your ultimate gear when you go shopping. The plastic can even be a best friend to a happy shopper.

Considering the times nowadays, this plastic seems to be the least practical option out there. It is actually the most convenient tool used for consumption when you are out of cash. It lures you to spend.

Is there anyway for your credit card to be useful for your saving endeavours?

Yes, actually there are ways that the plastic can be helpful. You CAN actually save money with that credit card.

0% Balance Transfers

If your present credit card has high interests, you can transfer your balance to one with a low-interest or no-interest at all. It can offer you a 0% interest for a certain period and then a lower regular rate later on. A 19% interest rate can be transferred to one with 16.1%. The 2.9% difference means a lot, especially in the long run.

Lower Interest Rates

Look for one with the lowest rate among others to further maximize having a credit card. This definitely spells savings. If you do not have a balance yet, it is best to look for a card without annual fees.

Take extra precautions, too, in assuming that the lowest interest rate is the best for you. Factor in your buying habits. You may be attracted to the low rates, but the end result may not be desirable if combined with the annual fees and the like.

Rewards Program

Reward points system and cash back programs are offered now. This can save you money. Maintaining a low balance despite your frequent buys will give you at most 5% off on purchases.

There are even cash rebates up to 5% when you use the credit card at certain gas stations, convenience stores and groceries. This can be automatically applied to your bill, the more you can feel the savings you are making.

Maximizing the Experience

To reap the rewards, you must avoid the drawbacks. A prudent person will definitely look for the best deals and grab it right away but with some caution.

Thus it is necessary that you read the details. Check the fees that may be charged and the penalty rates in case you delay. This may be the downside of the deal offered to you. For example, be careful of cash advance features of credit cards. Some of them can be very expensive. They can come with numerous fees and higher rates.

Be wary! Spending cannot be avoided at times. Just don't forget your goal, getting a good deal to save.

Saving Money And Energy At Home

Saving money is the game now if you really want to bank on a good future for you and your family. This is one definite way to ensure that you make yourself able and ready for whatever big plans you have ahead, be it getting a new house, buying a car, sending a kid to college or even a grand vacation.

There are many ways to save money. It can range from setting aside a portion of your monthly paycheck or avoiding the little temptations for you to spend. Make it your goal.

Start at Your Own Home

Saving money should be part of your way of life to make it most effective. It is best that the effort to save be shared by everyone in the family.

Little Efforts

Do not drive if you really don't have to. If you can, just take a walk or take the bus. Riding the bike can also be very good for your body. Have a car pool with friends or neighbors. You can also suggest doing errands together like doing the grocery store.

Avoid the little temptations that may come your way. It is naturally fine to reward yourself after a hard work every now and then, but do stay away from splurging. Cut back on your expenses.

Use Less and Save Energy

Electricity - Turn off appliances that are not used. Turn the TV off if the show is not worth it. Close the refrigerator after getting what you need. Use lower wattage bulb for rooms that do not need much lighting. These will definitely add more data to your savings!

Water - Check for any leaks in your pipes. Always make sure that the faucet is not dripping. Avoid long showers. Use a glass when brushing your teeth instead of leaving the faucet on.

Phone – Choose a provider that has savings plans especially for long-distance calls.

Gas - Have your car tuned up so you can save on gas. Get membership benefits also from stations. Fill up the tank when the prices go low. You can also do a research on gas saving cars if you have to purchase a new one. Turn off the air conditioning. If there is no need for that, simply keep the windows open. Enjoy the ride and the cool wind.

You may not realized this before, but your household's basic utilities can actually be your key to saving more money. This has a two-way benefit. You get to save some dollars for your family. You also contribute in addressing the energy crisis.

Saving Money And Part Time Jobs

Earning extra money for your future, that is definitely not a bad thing!

However, is it an easy thing? One definitely wants that for a stronger foundations for the future, but how can you manage?

Saving Money

One of the better ways to have a more secured future is to have more than enough money in your bank account, to be more liquid.

Time is Gold

Sometime in a day, you may find yourself with nothing to do. You can either take this time to rest, to sleep, to read a book or any of your favorite pastimes. Basically anything will do just to keep you sane and as long you do not have to spend too much money.

However, instead of looking for activities that will not be too costly to maintain, it is better to pursue things that can even help you earn money. If you have enough free time, consider taking a part-time job. More than saving money, you can even expect more dough into your savings!

Why Should I Get a Part-time Job?

- It can be a source for your extra money for your savings.
- You make good use of your free time.
- For a student, the experience can teach a lot about life and the real world.
- You can meet interesting people.
- There is the possibility of discovering new skills or passions.
- Getting a good part-time job can actually be a start to a more serious endeavour.

Getting a Part-time Job

It will be relatively easy to get a part-time job. You can look up the posters or newspapers. Inquire in different establishments for openings in part-time positions. Ask friends who may recommend you. You can even provide services of your own skills like tutorial, writing or painting.

The job may require from you a few hours of your week. It can be something you do in the afternoons, during the weekends, or during school breaks.

You may feel challenged by exploring this new possibility in your life. You will have to balance your part-time job with what you regularly do. Simply manage your work and time properly. Save time too. Do minor tasks when traveling or waiting. Give no room for distraction, procrastination or cramming.

As long as you keep track of your extra earnings and savings, in the long run, your part-time job will definitely help do wonders to your plans in the future.

Saving Money On Your Bills

I used to love going to the supermarket. But nowadays, I make my trips short and sweet. I have a list and stick to it. My trips to the supermarket made me realize that it's getting harder and harder to stretch that dollar. With all those bills that you have to pay in a month, you really can't do anything about it but to save.

I read once that it's not how much you earn that ensures a comfortable and happy future; but it's how much you save and keep saved that matters. That is why it is really important to save money especially when it comes to your monthly bills.

Some people do not just realize it but saving on their monthly bills can provide the best money-saving opportunity for them.

Here's how:

1. Turn off appliances and lights when not in use

The logic is basically simple. Why would you leave something turned on when nobody is going to use it? That's definitely a bad habit.

Hence, if you really want to cut back some on your electricity bill, always turn off the lights and your appliances when not in use.

2. Use energy-saving lights

Nowadays, saving on your electricity bill is not impossible because you can opt for energy-saving devices such as lights. Using these energy-saving lights such as fluorescent lights consumes lower amounts of energy but can still give the suitable amount of illumination.

3. Always check for the leaks

Water bills can create a mountain load of pile on your monthly dues if you do not check on the things that might cause your water bill to rise higher. You can prevent this by ensuring that every pipe is free from any leaks.

Some people do not just realize that single drops from leaking pipes could mean additional costs on your water bill.

4. Be more tech-savvy

Cut your phone bill to almost half by simply being tech-savvy. That is, opt for the emails and chatting services of the Internet instead of using your phone to call long distance to your relatives and friends.

5. Try to insulate your home

Insulating your home is a definite energy-saver, money-saver scheme. You will never know how much money you can save on your electricity bill when you start to insulate your home.

Indeed, cutting some of your bills can definitely allow you to save more money. You just have to be wise on your home and everything that you have in it.

Saving Money During The Holidays

With the hype that holidays usually bring, people always have the tendency to buy more and spend more without taking into account the consequences that their actions can bring.

Hence, it does not necessarily mean that because it is the holidays you have all the reason in this world to buy whatever you want and spend how much you want. Some people contend that it's just once a year, so better give what you have.

The problem is that giving something just for the spirit of the holidays does not mean you have to spend gold. You can still give something that will be deeply appreciated without having to spend more money.

Here's how:

1. Make a budget and stick to it

The problem with most people is that they find making a budget relatively easy but sticking to it is doubly hard. So what's the point of making a budget when you do not know how to conform to what you have stated in there?

Making and using your budget should always go hand in hand. Therefore, when you make your budget this holiday season, it is best that you follow the things that are written in it so that you would be able to save more money.

2. Live within your means

Of course, everybody would want to give gifts because that is what the holiday season calls for. However, it does not necessarily mean that you have to spend more than what you can afford.

The trick to saving more money is to always live within your means. Spending more than what you can afford will definitely bring more problems than you can afford to solve.

3. Personalize it!

As they say, it is the thought that counts. Hence, there are no better ways to show how much you have thought of those people this holiday season than making personalized gifts.

4. Shop and compare

It really pays to shop around and doubly better when you compare prices. You will never know which items are better priced than the others are when you do not compare their values.

The point here is that you should not be confined to one shopping portal. Try to look for other items, usually in thrift stores and consignment shops, where you can find the best items at a lower price.

Indeed, shopping for the holidays can be fun, but you don't have to be spendthrift. Nowadays, you really just have to be practical.

Saving Money On Clothes

Are you craving for the newest designer clothes, a pretty tank top, and that pretty dress? All this fashion comes at a price — you choose.

Buying clothes these days is always a choice between the designer-made outfit or those cheap but quality items that you could pull together and express your personality in many different ways.

Most experts contend that clothes can definitely make or break a person. They say that your personality is usually reflected on how you dress up. But it does not necessarily mean that good fashion would absolutely mean expensive clothes.

Hence, you can still make a remarkable fashion statement without having to spend hundreds or even thousands of dollars just for your clothes.

Here is a list of some money-saving tips when buying clothes that would turn other people's heads to you but would not definitely break your wallet.

1. Do the math

Choosing fashionable clothes can be really tricky, not unless you know how to do the math! So before you buy three sets of clothes that would cost you hundreds of dollars, try to go for the budget-friendly dozen of items that you can even match alternatively.

The number of expensive items that your money can buy is definitely doubled or even tripled when you buy cheaper ones but can still make a good fashion statement.

2. Know what you want

Saving money is definitely based on knowing what you want whenever you spend your money on something. If you know what you want, this means that you have researched the item, have compared them with the other items, you will be able to come up with the lowest price of the product.

3. Drive your way to a "thrift store"

Usually, these "thrift stores" are non-profit organizations. This means that they are usually operating for charity. They give their proceeds to some charitable institutions.

Hence, the prices of the clothes being sold in the thrift store are absolutely cheaper than the ones being sold in the department store. So that would mean many savings for you.

Best of all, you do not only get to save more money, you get to do some charity work as well.

The bottom line here is that when shopping for clothes, do not shop for the brand name, shop for the quality.

Nowadays, you just have to be practical. Better spend your money on more important things than those designer clothes.

Saving Money On Electricity

An electrical appliance that does not work at maximum capacity results in less than ideal performance and higher electricity bills. That is why it is best to save on electricity in order to save more money.

Here is how you can get everything saving up:

1. Keep your appliances clean and well maintained. Regular cleaning and maintenance keeps your appliances in top shape, hence, it will perform better and consumes lesser energy. Energy saved is money saved.

2. Have an annual checkup by a qualified service technician. This can reduce the appliance's operating costs by as much as 20%, extend the life of the system, and improve its safety and air quality.

3. When using air conditioners, it is best to establish your comfort temperature, and then setting your thermostat at that level permanently. This will definitely save on electric bills because the air conditioning unit takes less energy to cool air four to five degrees than it does to cool air eight to ten degrees.

4. Replace any items that may have been 10 years or older already. Old appliances are most likely not at their optimum efficiency. By replacing them, your electric bills may be cut by half.

5. If you experience a power outage, make sure you turn off the switch on your appliances and allow time to pass before turning the appliances on again when the power returns.

6. In refrigerators, do not overstuff compartments with bottles and plastic containers. Cool air must circulate freely to avoid overworking the condenser.

Also, try not to leave the door of your refrigerator as open as possible or open longer than what is needed. This will have the tendency to allow the cool air to break out.

7. Always try to look for the "energy saving" logo or notes whenever you buy your new appliances. Buying an appliance with a logo that states it consumes lower energy, it will definitely let you save more money on your electricity.

8. Always use energy saving lights or light bulbs. These energy saving lights or light bulbs usually last up to 12 times longer. Plus, energy saving light bulbs consume less energy. Hence, you will be able to save more money just by saving on electricity.

9. Use energy-saving facilities at home like energy-saving windows or energy-saving appliances. This will lessen the consumption of energy and, thus, will let you save on money.

For instance, use a "double-glazed" window instead of the ordinary window.

10. Use insulators at home. This will not let the warm or cool air out, and vice-versa.

Indeed, saving on electricity will definitely save more money.

Saving Money On Gifts

Giving gifts does not have to be spendthrift. As the old adage goes, "It is the thought that counts". This goes to show that people can start cutting back on gifts that would cost them hundreds of dollars. It is best to opt for things that may not be that expensive but would definitely bring joy and amusement to the one who will receive the gift.

So, if you want to give gifts but with a tight budget, worry no more because there are many ways to cut back on the prices but still be able to give gifts that will be deeply appreciated.

Start a Gift Closet

If you have not done this before, try to do it now. Shop for gifts the whole year-round. This would mean less hassle and less expense, a definite money-saver.

The point here is that if you do not plan in advance, you will end up spending more.

You could try buying gifts at bazaars, special sales, and out-of-town trips, which you can deposit in your gift closet. In this way, you can buy the items at a much lower price than it would be sold for during the holidays.

However, to make sure that you do not give the same gift twice, you should make an inventory of all your gifts. This will also allow you to keep tabs on what you have in your stock.

Alternatively, apart from stockpiling gifts, collect wrapping paper, ribbons, and other accents as well. A gift is better appreciated when it is beautifully wrapped.

Be Creative

Nothing could be more amusing than a gift that was specially made by the person who gave the gift. Personalizing you gifts is far better than commercially made items. In this way, you do not only create a smile to the one who will receive the gift but would also cut back a large amount from your expenses.

Organizing Tip

One of the best ways of saving money on gifts is to be organized with the process. That is, before going to the store to shop for the gifts, always bring with you a shopping list. It should be stated there the names of the person to whom you will give the gift and the budget for each person.

The bottom line is that gifts should not be expensive. What matters most is that you have thought of the person on that very special day and that's enough to make them feel they are special to you.

Saving Money On Medications

There is no such thing as a free lunch. Moreover, there is no such thing as free medication. Some time or another, all of us will need medical treatment. Whether it would be for simple colds or for serious illnesses, these things would hurt us and burn our pockets.

According to a recent study, Americans spend more money on medical expenses than any other nationality in the world. As prices get higher and life gets harder, saving some money from your medical expenses will definitely benefit you.

Here are some practical tips on how to cut your medical costs:

Mind Your Health

Prevention is always better than cure. Being fit and healthy seems to be a 21st century fad and it wouldn't hurt us if we join in the bandwagon. An analysis of the 1987 National Medical Expenditures Survey revealed that people who are more active spend less on medical expenses than those who live lethargic lives. The analysis equated the benefit of being physically active to $330 (1987 dollar value) per person.

For smokers and drinkers, reducing cigarette and alcohol consumption is an option which you may find feasible. You will not only reduce future medical costs but also reduce direct costs from purchasing these products.

Go Generic

Taking generic drugs is the way to go. Patents are used by manufacturers to be able to set a price so as to recover their costs in developing their products. But these patents don't last forever and sooner or later, generic versions of these drugs will be available. Generic drugs are basically the same as the branded ones in terms of ingredients and quality.

Going generic can save you a lot of money. According to the Association of Chain Drug Stores, the generic drugs are priced at $24 on the average in 2004, while the average price of the branded ones is $96 dollars.

Deal with your Doctor

Take time out to discuss things with your doctor, for this can also save you a lot of cash. Don't be shy to ask him about the possible alternatives that you can take. Ask him if there is a generic drug that you can take if he prescribes you a branded drug. If you are going to have surgery, try to schedule wisely, so as to prevent overstaying in the hospital. And most importantly, do as you are told. If he asks you to quit your vice, quit it. If he tells you to be active, then you'd better be!

Medical expenses can really dig a hole in your pocket. Try to be wise in your medical transactions and more importantly, take care of your health.

Saving Money On School Expenses

Whenever the school season is just around the corner, there's only one thing that parents are thinking about - the impending costs. Education is a primary right and a pertinent need of every child but it can become very costly. Availing of scholarships and education grants for your children is the best way to get them through schooling. But of course, only a small percentage of children can be given these privileges.

There are simple and effective measures that parents can employ in cutting the costs of their children's schooling, especially during the back-to-school season. Most often, these measures are often taken for granted, but don't miss out!

Organize and Save

Keep an inventory of your children's school supplies and keep it organized. If you are not organized, you will be spending more money on replenishing your supplies. Small things like pencils and crayons may not cost too much, but if you replenish your supplies unnecessarily, you are losing valuable money.

You should also try involving the kids when making the inventory. This will give them a sense of ownership for their things and would know where to take and put their things.

Tax Holidays

Tax holidays are often offered by many states during the back-to-school season. Price ceilings will be put on different school gears. You might want to do a little research and ask about the schedule and the details of the tax holidays in your area.

Bulk Buying

It's a basic economic principle - "the more you buy, the more you save". Well, this is applicable if you are buying a specific item which you will really need in the near future. In buying pencils, for example, you might want to buy a box rather than buying one for each of your kids. Face it, you will be needing to replenish these after some time, so might as well avail of the lower price by buying in bulk.

Transportation

You might want to consider buying your child a bicycle for him to bring to school. This, of course, is not always feasible. Finding a cheap and safe way to bring your children to school daily is an important thing. Car pools and school transportation services are options that you can look at.

Snacks

Whenever you have the time and energy to prepare food for your children, do so. You will not only be saving on the pocket money that you will give to them but you are also secured that your children are eating healthy and safe meals.

Getting your children through school is a hard task and a costly one. Saving money through practical and simple means can assist you in this endeavour. The benefits will eventually add up to bring a brighter future to your children.

Saving Money On The Bank

Many of us think that putting our money in the bank is a secure and wise way of saving. Yes, this is true if we are wise in dealing with banks. Banks are not charitable institutions, these are profit-driven entities which charge different kinds of fees and do all sorts of schemes to take away some of your money. The savings that you can get in being wise in making bank transactions can add up after some time and let you use your money where you want to.

Here are some tips on how to effectively save money in the bank:

Mind the Opportunity Cost

Think about the factors that are affecting your money in the bank. Are there fees that the bank is asking you to pay for keeping and using your own money? How much? Are they requiring a minimum balance for holding an account? You might be interested in other alternatives that are available out there, waiting for your investment. You should always factor in the opportunities that you are deprived of because you are putting your money in the bank. You might also be interested in taking a look into the terms of other banks. Probably the bank that can best suit your needs is out there waiting for you.

Book Balancing

Always bear in mind to have your checkbooks balanced at the end of every month. Issuing bounced checks can cost you a lot. The average fee for issuing checks with insufficient funds is $20. If you are not aware of the problem, you can easily issue several bounced checks in a certain period of time and this is very costly indeed.

Tame the ATM Machines

The best practice in using ATM machines is to avoid using ATM machines of other banks. This way, you will save on ATM fees. However, it wouldn't hurt if you also knew the ATM machines of other banks which do not charge fees.

E-banking

With the advent of globalization, everything is becoming electronic. This is also true in the banking world and technology is quickly becoming a benchmark of competition. E-banking can save you some money from transportation costs and more importantly, it will save you time. The time you spend waiting at the bank can be used for some other productive activities.

Truly, putting your money in the bank is a wise way of saving money, but only if you are wise enough to prevent the bank from chipping away your wealth. In saving, it is not only the benefits such as annual returns which you should consider, you should always think about the costs involved in the process.

Saving Money On Tuition Fees

As soon as their child is born, parents can start saving up for their children's college education.

With tuition fees climbing up yearly, it is better to have a sound financial plan so that it would not be difficult for you to send your kids off to college when they grow up.

Aside from the cash that you have saved yourself, here are the top 3 sources that can help you get your kids through college:

1. Scholarship grants
2. Part-time jobs
3. Financial aids

These are good alternative sources for your children to start off on their college education.

But as a parent, you would not want to fall in those long lines for financial aid or let your child work himself to death just to have money for tuition and other expenses.

Here are some ways on how you can have a jump start at shaving off those hard-earned bucks for your child's college education:

1. The earlier, the better.

Start investing your money as soon as your child is born.

First, put the savings or investments under your name.

Later on, decide whether you want to transfer the account to your child's name by the time he or she turns 15. This way, you will have minimal taxes, if at all.

However, you need to be careful when transferring account names.

Some states require a total turnover of funds once your child turns 18 or 21. This is also ineffective if, in the future, you apply for financial aid.

Also remember that tuition fees 10 or 15 years from now may double or even triple the current rates.

2. Establish a trust fund for your child.

This is a very wise plan for a child's parents or relatives to invest in.

A trust fund is similar to a time-deposit where the money will be given to your child after a certain number of years.

After the designated time, the fund may be received in one lump sum or through an instalment basis.

When building up a trust fund, check out details like the interest rates, taxes and withdrawal restrictions.

All in all, you need to approximate the costs of tuition fees, dorm room, meals, books, and other expenses that may come up.

Make sure that you invest money wisely as your child grows.

By the time that there are only two or three years to go before you send your son or daughter off to college, "lock" an ample amount of the funds by investing them in low-risk bonds to ensure that you will get to have enough for them to start their college education.

Secret Budgeting Family Money

The high cost of living in today's society, wherever you may be, has made budgeting a priority among families. In today's inflationary world, nothing is more important than knowing how to wisely spend the meagre income that you get.

Financial problems usually arise due to lack of proper budgeting skills, or failure to keep to the proposed budget. No matter how much income you may have, it is still important to keep track of your assets and liabilities, your earnings and expenses.

It is ironic but a person who earns thousands will have the same problems with the person who earns by the hundreds. Most often, different kinds of people, with diverse income levels, have budgeting problems. Others who may have been successful in making a budget, usually fail to keep within such a budget.

A budget refers to a financial plan, taking the incoming and outgoing monetary resources into consideration. A good budget should not only mean a balance or equity between income and expenditures. It also means lesser expenses, and making an allowance for savings.

If you earn a thousand dollars per month, you should map out all the necessary expenses you will have to incur during the month such as payment for your house, food and transportation. Of course, this is presuming that your tax liabilities have already been settled. What remains after you deduct your total expenses from your income is your savings.

What you do with your savings will make a difference later on, when the need arises. You can choose to keep your savings in a piggy bank or place it in a bank where there is minimum interest rate but at least your money is safe from you and from intruders. With a bigger savings, you can get the services of a financial adviser who can give you higher-yielding investment options

Here are tips to make sure that you keep within the family budget:

1. Maintain a logbook where you can list your income and expense account on a weekly or monthly schedule.

2. Buy your groceries at one time. To do this, make a list of all the things that you would need for your target period and purchase them at one time. Sometimes, there are discounts if you buy by the dozen so take advantage of this.

3. Avoid going to the supermarket and shops if you do not need to buy necessary items. This will keep you from making unnecessary purchases and keep you from straying away from your budget.

4. Think twice before you buy something. By doing this, you will realize that it is not really a necessity but a whim.

Self Control And Saving Money

Self-control is one of the many virtues that is something that can be learned by each and every person. And learning it will prove to be very significant in the way people handle their finances. Possessing a sense of self-control somehow helps people to put aside money instead of spending it. It helps people to resist the terrible "itch" they get to spend money the moment they get hold of it.

This is a common pitfall for most people. Often, when people come into a certain amount of money, they have this tendency to rush out and instantly satisfy the irresistible urge to splurge on anything they lay their eyes on. This is a very dangerous mistake. Sometimes people fail to recognize the idea that the future has to be considered, too, whenever spending and savings enter the picture.

The cliché "nothing is constant" still rings true until today. The stuff people see now as shiny and new will fade and rust away later. And patience and self-control makes people realize and think about the many other more important things that requires more of people's concern, specifically money-wise.

A person's financial success starts with a conscious effort to control one's expenditures and save up for the future.

Realizing the high correlation of self-control and saving money, the next question is, how do we start learning and acquire this virtue of self-control, which seems so elusive? Well, there are many ways which people often take for granted. Here are some of the less complicated ones that are easier to follow. Learn them, and hope they grow on you. Try to apply these easy steps in your daily living and surely they will bear you wonderful fruits on your way to financial stability and security.

1. Do not purchase items on impulse. Consider thinking if you really need the item, or maybe you can still put it off for later when you really have the need for it.

2. Identify your needs from wants. You wouldn't want to spend so much on something that you may regret doing so in the future.

3. Look for a person who can serve as a role model for you and adapt a financial life similar to what he does. In this way, self-control will seem very easy when you see that others are actually doing it.

Self Discipline And Saving Money

A great way to save money is to be aware of the fact that one has the power to define the state of his finances specifically through a conscious effort of disciplining the way one spends and controlling one's expenditures.

Self-discipline will most definitely be the key to reducing one's debts therefore increasing the possibility of growing one's savings. And in the long run, improve one's standard of living.

According to money management book author Robert Hastings, "Undisciplined money, usually spells undisciplined person". Therefore, if one notices how his hard-earned money seems to slip away so darned easy, then it is about time that he rethinks his ways and try to discipline his unpleasant spending habits.

One of the essential keys to successful money management, specifically saving money is to possess proper attitude. Self-discipline is at the topmost of this proper attitudes list, of course.

Only with self-discipline that people recognize that they do have the freedom and power to do the right thing over doing as their impulses dictate.

Sounds complicated? Well, not really. Knowing fully the fantastic rewards of disciplined money in a disciplined person's hands should be motivation enough for one to do all that is humanly possible to achieve that elusive financial stability everyone hopes for.

Here are some helpful money saving tips.

1. Realize that the most convenient method of building one's wealth is through saving money. Money is the only sensible material to save.

2. Focus expenditures on the things one needs. Live day-by-day knowing that you have enough.

3. Avoid buying on impulse. Take your time when buying, especially the expensive items. If you really need it, it would most definitely not slip your mind. Otherwise, if you go along forgetting all about it, then it isn't really worth the money you have to spend on it at all.

4. Credit card debts hold the number one slot as the cause for financial drains these days. Control your spending by using your credit cards less. Or for unavoidable circumstances when you really have to use the credit card, consider using the ones that charge less interest. Then dump the high interest ones for good.

No matter how you look at it, saving money is so easy to do. A little bit of imagination, some creativity and a lot of self-discipline will take you a long way in keeping hold of your hard-earned money.

Setting Up A Family Budget

For some, the idea of a budget is often a blur. It is frustrating to see how hard it is to do a budget and realizing that with one wrong purchase, you can actually ruin the entire thing. And this has been a perennial headache for most homemakers.

It is about time to overhaul the way people look at budgeting. It can actually be a great way to keep track of your family's expenditures and help you evaluate the things that you spend the lion's share of the family's earnings on.

What is a budget? A budget is a tool for handling your finances by controlling the family's expenditures in a way that money is enough for paying up bills, and still ensuring that savings are set aside for future expenses - vacations, or children's education, or even for retirement.

Try these simple steps in preparing a no fret family budget, and see the benefits of intelligent spending.

1. Gather three months of your pay stubs and get your average monthly earnings.

2. Get out three months of your monthly bills. Do this for the fixed expenses like the rent, phone bill, car payments and other loans that come monthly. Add them up and get the average. Do the same for other expenses like groceries, and credit card bills.

3. Evaluate the results of your computations. Looking at your average monthly earnings against your monthly fixed expenses and other monthly expenses, think of some ways to economize. Cut back on some items that are somehow unnecessary.

4. Knowing the facts of your income and expenses, develop a family budget and try to stick to this monthly budget.

5. Now that you have a monthly budget, set up a savings account. Save up by making regular deposits to this account.

6. Keep track of this monthly family budget just to see if it is working for you. Try to fine-tune the "rough edges" of this budget as you go along.

7. If you can get hold of a personal budgeting software or spreadsheet application to keep record of your budget, the better. This will make organizing your expenses very easy.

These are the basic steps in developing and implementing a no fret, easy to stick to monthly family budget. Of course each family has diverse needs and wants. You have the freedom to develop your own monthly family budget, depending on your family's financial background and needs. No matter how you do it, just focus on the end result, which is building a savings that leads to a bright and financially stable future for your family.

Student Money Saving Tips

It is easy to get caught in the rush of things when you are in college. In the midst of studying, part-time jobs, socializing and extracurricular activities that you have, you are most likely to forget one of the most important things, which is straightening out your finances.

Here are some tips on how you can save money as a student:

1. Plan ahead.

If possible, do this even before you move into your dorm room.

Check if you are eligible for scholarships and other grants before signing up for any form of student loan.

Construct a cash flow. First, where do you expect to get money from? Make a list of your "income", be it from your parents, your student loan or your part-time job.

Then forecast your expected monthly or weekly expenses for food, books, etc. Once you have set aside a budget, be strict with yourself and stick to it.

You will never know what unexpected expenses would come your way so it is better to have a downfall for financial emergencies.

2. Save on food.

One of the major expenses that you have as a student which you might have ignored when you were still living with your parents is your food allowance. Avoid eating at fast food outlets, as this is most likely to ruin your budget. Pack your lunch and plan your meals as much as you can.

3. Take full advantage of student discounts.

Those ID's in your wallet are not just for show. Student ID's and memberships in organizations are honored in several establishments which offer discounts.

Also, patronize a certain establishment regularly and you are bound to get bonus cards for being a loyal customer.

4. Use your cash as much as you can.

Since you already have a draft of the items where you will spend your money, it is easier to monitor your cash flow. Avoid using your debit card when you have cash with you. Use your credit cards or write checks only in emergencies. Having debit cards, credit cards and checks handy might lead you to overspend.

5. Keep yourself busy.

Join clubs according to your field of interest.

Keeping busy will let your mind wander and help you stay away from things that you are likely to spend money on when you get bored. Examples of these are snacks, movie tickets or game rentals.

You will be surprised at the amount of money that you will actually save by spending less on luxury items, following your budget plan and saving for financial emergencies that you are most likely to get as a college student.

Teaching Teens To Save Money

Parents mostly complain that teenagers do not listen to them. The opposite is true when it comes to advice regarding 'money matters'. Teens actually welcome their parent's input about their finances.

In the past few years, teenagers have earned billions of dollars with part-time and summer jobs.

Some have spent most of what they earned, while others saved most or even all of it for a big purchase, or for their college education.

Kids these days are becoming more and more aware of their family's source of income and financial status. They apply these money-spending principles when they venture out on their own.

Thus, it becomes more of a parent's responsibility to start "training" their teenage kids to use their money wisely.

Here are some ways on how you, as a parent, can teach your teens to save those hard-earned bucks:

1. Lead by example.

With your lifestyle, the children will see how you spend your money.

If they see you allotting a certain amount for a specific household need, they will eventually do the same when they get to earn their own keep.

2. Help your teens get a bank account.

Establishing a bank account under their name would give them an instant financial responsibility.

Sit down and explain to them how to manage their own account, and the "rewards" that they get once they save enough.

Their savings could go to their college tuition, or a big purchase like a car.

Additionally, it gives them a sense of accomplishment once they have saved up, with something concrete to show for it.

You may check out the special benefits that banks offer for teens who open their accounts at such an early age.

3. Construct a "spending plan".

Once they hear the word 'budget', teens tend to cringe at the mere thought of having to restrict the spending of their money.

Instead, you and your teen son or daughter could build a "spending plan". This would get them excited, and think of ways on how they can wisely spend their savings.

Also, have them list down their earnings versus their expenses.

Let them know the difference between the items that they need and the luxury items that they want, which they can actually do without.

4. Make a "mock" investment in the stock market.

Make them aware of the options that they have financially.

Casually introduce to them the business part of your daily newspapers and have them make "mock" investments for companies who manufactures products that they like.

Monitor the stocks together and this would give them another option of investing their money in the future.

Teach Your Kids To Save Money

A lot of teens nowadays do not understand the value of earning and spending money. They were not oriented that investing is necessary even if they are still students. As parents, you play a crucial role in this area.

You should be able to teach your kids on how to save money. They should be able to understand the concept of money and investment as early as childhood. This will prepare them to learn money management, as they grow old.

Here are some tips on how you can teach your children how to save money:

1. Your children should be educated of the meaning of money. Once your children have learned how to count, that is the perfect time for you teach them the real meaning of money. You should be consistent and explain to them in simple ways and do this

frequently so that they may be able to remember what you taught them.

2. Always explain to them the value of saving money. Make them understand its importance and how it will impact their life. It is important that you entertain questions from them about money and you should be able to answer them right away.

3. When giving them their allowances. You need to give them their allowances in denominations. Then you can encourage them that they should keep a certain bill for the future. You can motivate them to do this by telling them that the money can be saved and they can buy new pair of shoes or the toys they want once they are able to save.

4. You can also teach them to work for money. You can start this at your own home. You can pay them fifty cents to one dollar every time they clean their rooms, do the dishes or feed their pets. This concept of earning little money will make them think that money is something they have worked for and should be spent wisely.

5. You can teach them to save money by giving them piggy banks where they can put coins and wait until they get full. You can also open bank accounts for them and let them deposit money from their allowance. You should always show them how much they have earned to keep them motivated.

Money and saving is not something that is learned by children in one sitting. You should be patient in teaching them and relating the value of money in all of their activities. Children will learn this easily if you are patient and consistent in guiding them and encouraging them in this endeavour.

Temptations And Money

Saving money and financial management is very crucial in one's life. Money is very important in order to survive in this world but only a few people know how to manage their household budget properly. Many people have a hard time saving money even if it is for their own good.

Most of the time, you may be motivated to save money but there are times when temptations come your way and before you know it, you have already spent the amount that was supposed to be added to your savings account. Here are some helpful tips on how you can avoid temptations and be able to save money:

1. Try hard to avoid those things that keep you from saving. If you are fond of buying shoes even if you don't really need them, try very hard to stay away from them. Keep yourself away from shoe stores so that you will not be tempted to buy one.

2. When going to grocery stores. Always bring the exact amount and bring with you a grocery list. If you have limited money in your pocket when in grocery stores, you will be forced to buy only those important things that you need. Preparing a grocery list will also help you get organized and will help you in deciding the things that need to be prioritized.

3. Go to the malls only when needed. Do not go shopping if you do not need anything important to buy. Window-shopping will only tempt you to buy the dress you saw in the boutique even if you don't really need it.

4. Do not bring with you your credit cards all the time. Having a credit card in your pocket will only tempt you to buy things that are not necessary. This will also help you lower your balances and have a good credit score.

5. You may want to save money in the bank or invest in time deposits. You will not be tempted to get money from the bank every time you need cash, if they are placed in a time deposit account.

6. You may also want to consider consulting a financial advisor. There are a lot of programs that offer these services for free. They may be able to help you and give you advice on how you can avoid temptations and save more money.